BODY SYSTEMS

Reproduction and Birth

Angela Royston

RIGBY
INTERACTIVE
LIBRARY

Interiors designed by Inklines and Small House Design
Illustrations by Catherine Ward, except:
Peter Bull Art Studio, p. 9 and p. 11; John Bovosier, p. 20.

Printed in the United Kingdom

00 99 98 97 96
10 9 8 7 6 5 4 3 2 1

Library of Congress Cataloging-in-Publication Data
Royston, Angela.
    Birth and reproduction / Angela Royston.
      p. cm. – (Body systems)
Includes bibliographical references and index.
Summary: Describes the male and female reproductive systems, how babies are conceived
and born, and how genes determine the individual characteristics of each person.
    ISBN 1-57572-099-X (library)
    1. Human reproduction – Juvenile literature. 2. Childbirth – Juvenile literature.
[1. Reproduction. 2. Childbirth.]
1. Title. II. Series: Body systems (Crystal Lake, Ill.)
QP251.5.R69 1997
612.6 – dc20   96-27553
                                                                  CIP
                                                                  AC

Acknowledgments
The publisher would like to thank the following for permission to reproduce photographs:
Bubbles: p. 19 (C. Fulton), p. 26 (bottom – Ian West), p. 25, p. 28 (F. Rombout); Collections/Anthea
Sieveking, p. 6, p. 22; Sally and Richard Greenhill Photo Library, p. 13, p. 28; Rex Features, p. 7, p. 27;
Science Photo Library, p. 4, p. 8, p. 9, p. 10, p. 11, p. 12, p. 14, p. 16, p. 17 (both), p. 21 (both), p. 23
(both); Frank Spooner Pictures, p. 29. Commissioned photograph p. 26 (top), Trevor Clifford.

Every effort has been made to contact copyright holders of any material reproduced in this book.
Any omissions will be rectified in subsequent printings if notice is given to the publisher.

Note to the Reader
Some words in this book are printed in **bold** type. This indicates that the word is listed in the
glossary on pages 30–31. This glossary gives a brief explanation of words that may be new to you.

Visit Rigby's Education Station® on the World Wide Web at http://www.rigby.com

Contents

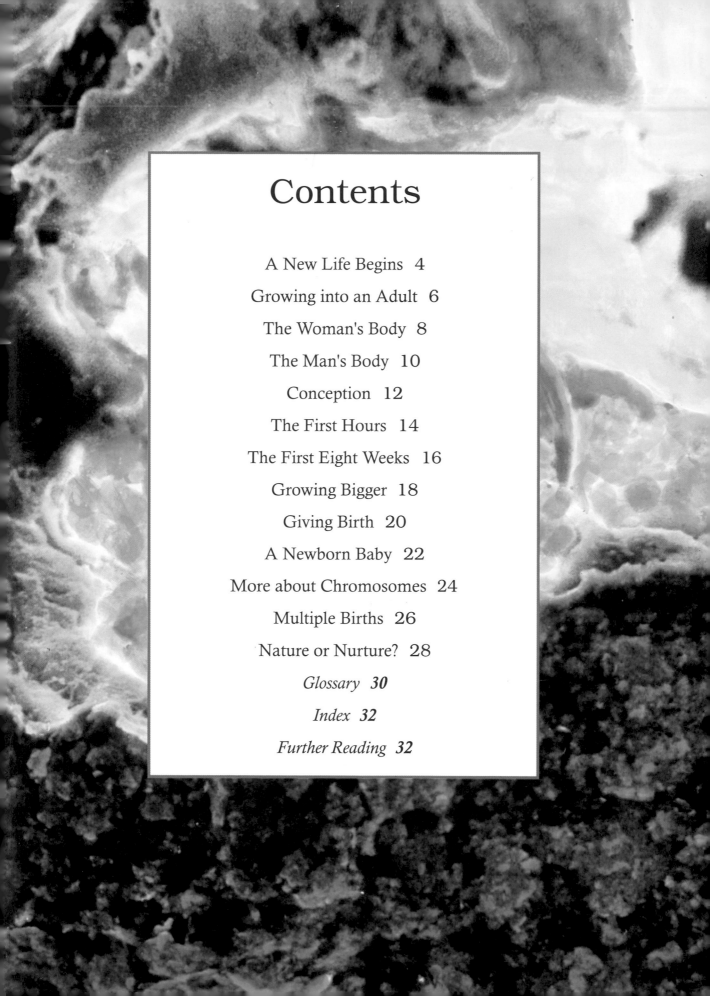

A New Life Begins 4

Growing into an Adult 6

The Woman's Body 8

The Man's Body 10

Conception 12

The First Hours 14

The First Eight Weeks 16

Growing Bigger 18

Giving Birth 20

A Newborn Baby 22

More about Chromosomes 24

Multiple Births 26

Nature or Nurture? 28

Glossary **30**

Index **32**

Further Reading **32**

A New Life Begins

Every time a baby is born it seems like a miracle. An entirely new human being, different from everyone else, has appeared. Yet the beginning of a new life is an incredibly common event. All around us new plants, insects, and other animals are sprouting and growing. All kinds of living things must reproduce if their kind is to survive. Every living thing has **organs,** whose job is to create new life.

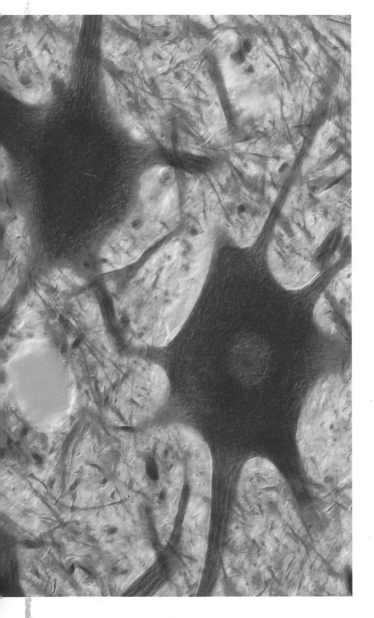

Males and females

It takes a man and a woman to make a new human life. Males and females have different sexual organs—the man's sexual organs produce male **sex cells** and the woman's produce female sex cells. A male sex cell must join with a female sex cell to make the first cell of a new person.

This first **cell** divides and multiplies to form all the different kinds of cells in the body. For nine months the growing **fetus** develops inside the mother. By the time the baby is ready to be born, the single cell has multiplied into two billion cells, making a new and completely separate human being!

◄ *Cells are the building blocks of all living things. This photograph shows what nerve cells in the brain look like under a microscope.*

Growing and changing

Babies go on growing and changing. Their heads are large compared with their bodies at first, and their arms and legs are short. As a baby becomes a child, its body grows faster than its head, and its arms and legs grow faster still.

When children reach **puberty,** a new set of changes occurs. Their bodies become more adult and their sexual organs begin to mature. The changes mean that one day they too will be able to produce children.

13 years

7 years

2½ years

6 months

19 years

adult

▲ *Children not only grow bigger as they get older; their proportions change, too.*

Did you know?

About 137 million babies are born every year—that's 258 every minute. Every kind of living thing has to reproduce to survive.

Growing into an Adult

Puberty is the time when you start to change into an adult. Puberty usually begins sometime between the ages of 11 and 14 for girls and between 13 and 16 for boys. Both girls and boys grow rapidly during puberty, and the proportions of their body parts change. The sexual, or **reproductive, organs** begin to work. These changes are brought about by **hormones,** which affect the emotions, too.

◀ *Teenagers often spend hours sitting around and talking. Their emotions and interests as well as their bodies are developing.*

Physical changes

During puberty a girl's breasts begin to grow, her waist becomes smaller, and her hips wider. Her **ovaries** start to release eggs and her **periods** begin. A boy's shoulders and chest broaden. His **penis** becomes thicker and longer, and his **testicles** produce **sperm.**

A boy's voice becomes much deeper around the time of puberty. In fact, his **vocal cords,** which produce the sound, grow so quickly that the **muscles** in charge of them sometimes get confused. The pitch of his voice wobbles unpredictably between high and low until the muscles find the right tension.

Both girls and boys find new hair growing on parts of their bodies, particularly between the legs and under the arms. Girls also notice hair growing on their legs for the first time, and boys notice it on their faces and on their chests.

Changing attitudes

Puberty doesn't only bring changes in the body. It also affects emotions and attitudes. Teenagers become acutely aware of how they look and often start to notice an attraction to members of the opposite sex. They slowly become more independent and responsible for themselves and others.

Parents and teenagers often argue about how independent teenagers are ready to be! Some feel they can assert their independence only by being rebellious.

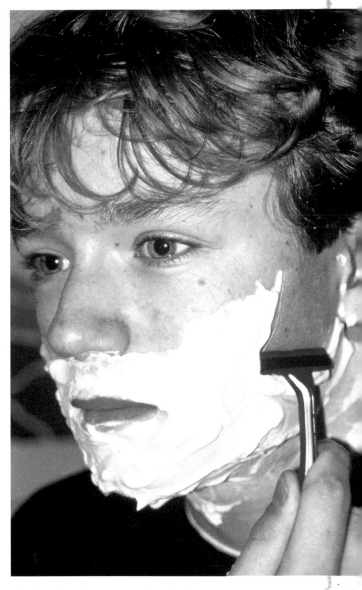

▲ For a boy, having to shave is just one of the outcomes of puberty.

Did you know?

Girls have just as many body hairs as boys, even on their faces. As boys grow older, however, their body hair becomes thicker, longer, and more noticeable. Many boys consider the appearance of facial hair a sign of manhood.

The Woman's Body

The female sex organs are mainly hidden inside the abdomen. The sex organs have two main purposes—to produce eggs and provide a safe place (the **womb**) for the fetus to develop. The eggs are stored in the ovaries, which are linked to the womb by the two thin **Fallopian tubes**. The womb is connected to the outside of the body by the **cervix** and **vagina**. The opening to the vagina is in folds of skin between the legs.

An egg is released

Every month the female **reproductive system** gets ready to make a new baby. An egg matures in one of the ovaries and is released into the Fallopian tube. The egg will live only 12 to 24 hours unless it is **fertilized** in the tube by a sperm. As the egg travels down the tube, the lining of the womb becomes thicker. It is ready for a fertilized egg to embed itself. If the egg has not been fertilized, it dies.

Periods

The unused lining and egg are then washed out of the womb in a slow flow of blood through the vagina. The flow of blood is called **menstruation,** or more simply, a **period.** It usually lasts about a week, and there may be some pain at the beginning. Women wear sanitary napkins or insert a **tampon** into the vagina to absorb the blood. The napkin or tampon has to be changed every few hours. At the end of the period, a new egg begins to mature and the whole cycle happens again.

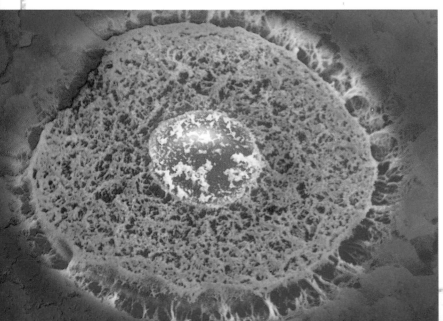

◄ An egg (the green ball) leaves the ovary to begin its journey down the Fallopian tube. The photo has been colored to show the egg more clearly.

The first period

A girl is born with all the eggs she will ever have already formed in her ovaries. But the eggs do not start to mature, and a girl's sexual organs do not start working until her early teens. At first her periods may occur haphazardly, but as her body gets used to the monthly cycle, her periods become more regular.

► *This photo shows an egg (red ball in the center) entering the Fallopian tube. It is magnified about 2,000 times.*

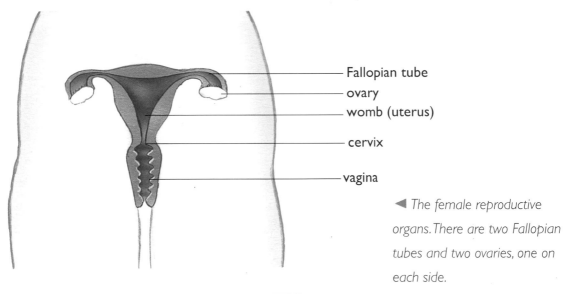

Fallopian tube
ovary
womb (uterus)
cervix
vagina

◄ *The female reproductive organs. There are two Fallopian tubes and two ovaries, one on each side.*

Did you know?

A baby girl is born with about 300,000 eggs in her ovaries. By the time she is 12 years old only about 10,000 are still capable of being fertilized. Of these, just over 400 will be released, one by one, until the woman is about 50. Around this age, usually, the ovaries stop releasing eggs.

The Man's Body

A man's sex **organs** are mainly outside his body. They have two functions: to make sperm, or male sex cells, and to place the sperm inside the woman's body. Sperm are made in the testicles, two organs contained in the **scrotum,** a pouch behind the penis. Sperm leave the man's body through the penis.

A long journey

The testicles hang outside the body to keep them cool — if sperm become too warm they die. Sperm travel to the penis through a long tube called the **vas deferens**. On the way they become mixed with a fluid called **semen.** When a man is ready to have sex, his penis becomes stiff. During sexual intercourse, muscles contract at the base of the penis. This makes the semen and sperm spurt out or ejaculate.

During puberty a boy's penis may become stiff and ejaculate sperm while he is asleep. This is called a "wet dream."

The penis

The penis is not only a sex organ. It also empties **urine** from the **bladder.** There is no danger of these two functions getting mixed up. When the penis becomes stiff, the tube from the bladder is blocked off.

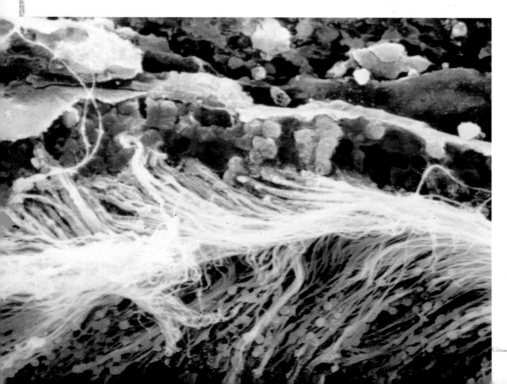

◄ *This photo has been color tinted. The fine purple strands are the tails of sperm being made in a tiny tube in the testicle. The sperm are then stored in the* **epididymis** *alongside the testicle.*

Foreskin

The tip of the penis is protected by a fold of skin called the **foreskin**. When the penis becomes erect, the foreskin slides back. Some people believe the foreskin should be removed. This operation, known as circumcision, is usually done soon after birth if it is done at all.

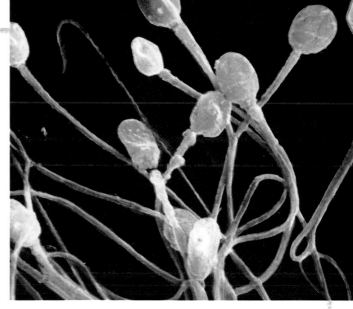

▲ *A sperm looks a bit like a tadpole. The head carries the sex cell, and the long tail thrashes to and fro to move the sperm along.*

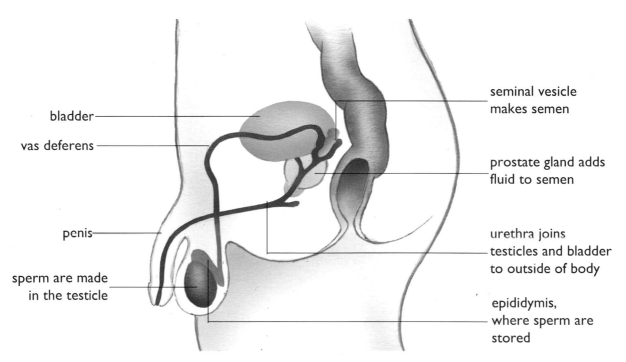

bladder

vas deferens

penis

sperm are made in the testicle

seminal vesicle makes semen

prostate gland adds fluid to semen

urethra joins testicles and bladder to outside of body

epididymis, where sperm are stored

▲ *The male reproductive organs.*

Did you know?

Sperm are tiny. About 5,000 of them laid head to tail would measure an inch. After puberty the testicles make about 200 million sperm every day. They can survive for several weeks in the epididymis before they die and turn to liquid.

Conception

Conception, the start of a new life, occurs when a man's sperm joins with a woman's egg as it travels down one of her Fallopian tubes. How does the sperm get to the unfertilized egg? The man and woman have **sexual intercourse,** or "make love." The man puts his penis inside the woman's vagina and ejaculates sperm, which then race to reach the egg.

Making love

When a couple wants to make love, or have sexual intercourse, the man and woman become sexually excited. As this happens, blood vessels in the man's penis fill with blood to make the penis stiff. The woman's vagina produces a slippery fluid that allows the penis to enter the vagina easily. As the couple is making love, the man ejaculates, and semen and sperm spurt into the woman's vagina. After this, the penis becomes limp again.

The sperm race

Sperm use their long tails to swim up the vagina and into the womb. About 500 million sperm start the race at high speed. These tiny cells have to swim upstream and have just

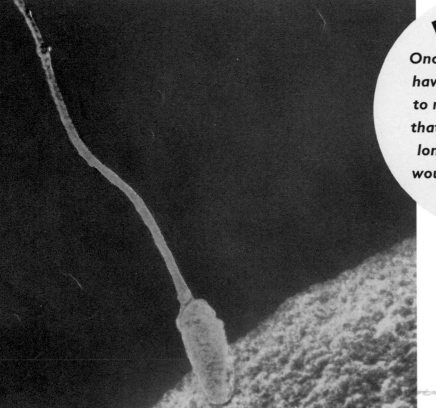

Did you know?

Once inside the vagina, sperm have to travel about 6 inches to reach the egg. Remember that sperm are only .002 inch long. The equivalent for you would be swimming about 70 laps in a pool!

◄ *The moment of fertilization. The sperm (blue) has just broken through the egg's cell wall (pink). Its long tail stays outside — only the head joins with the egg.*

a few hours to reach the egg before they die. Only a few hundred of the millions of sperm released during sexual intercourse reach the woman's Fallopian tube, and only one of these sperm can fertilize the egg. Each of the woman's eggs is surrounded by layers of cells or the cell **membrane**. Sperm try to fight their way into the egg. At last one sperm breaks through the membrane, which then thickens so that no other sperm can enter. The egg has now been fertilized, and a new life has begun.

◄ A couple can express love for each other in many ways. They can show their love by speaking and listening to each other, sharing what they have, helping each other, and doing things they enjoy.

The First Hours

As soon as a sperm joins with an egg, something amazing happens. The new cell begins to copy itself and a few hours later splits into two cells. Every 12 hours or so, the number of cells doubles: the two cells become four cells, the four become eight, and so on. By the time the fertilized egg reaches the womb, it has become a ball of about 64 cells. To survive, it must attach itself in the lining of the womb. There the cells continue to divide. They start to form different kinds of cells now, organizing themselves into the **embryo** of a new human being.

Blueprint for life

How can different kinds of cells form from just one cell? The answer lies in **chromosomes**. Chromosomes carry a set of coded instructions that tell each kind of cell what to do and how to reproduce itself. The **nucleus** of the egg and sperm each contain a half set of chromosomes, which join together to make a new combination of chromosomes. Before a cell divides it copies the chromosomes so that each new cell has an identical set.

◄ *This magnified and artificially colored photo shows a cluster of cells four days after the egg was fertilized and just before it implants itself in the wall of the womb.*

A question of looks

In addition to telling each kind of cell what to do, chromosomes decide how you will look—the color of your eyes, the shape of your nose, and so on. They also decide which sex you will be.

Since you have inherited half your chromosomes from your mother and half from your father, you share some characteristics with each of them. You may not think that you look much like your parents or brothers and sisters, but no doubt other people say you do. Incredible though it may seem, the way you look now was determined from the moment the first cell formed.

Did you know?

From the moment of conception, you had some 100,000 genes, or pieces of information that tell your cells how to grow. About half of them are common to all human beings. The other half make you different from all other human beings.

▼ Before a cell divides, it copies the chromosomes to form two complete sets. The cell then divides into two so that each cell has an identical set of chromosomes.

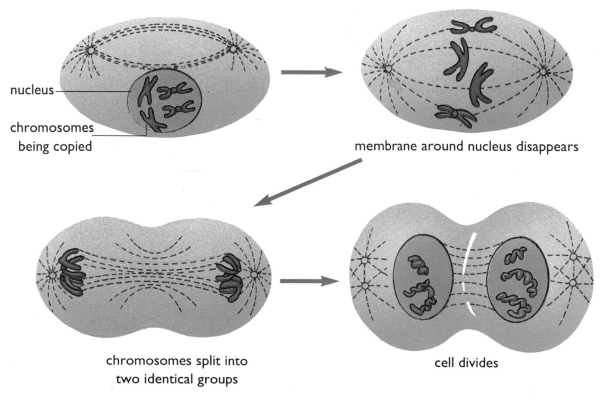

nucleus

chromosomes being copied

membrane around nucleus disappears

chromosomes split into two identical groups

cell divides

The First Eight Weeks

In the first eight weeks of life the human embryo changes from a cluster of **cells** to the recognizable shape of a human being. It spends its time in the womb floating in a bag of liquid. It doesn't need to breathe or eat, because all the oxygen and food it needs until it is born comes from the mother.

The growing embryo

Three weeks after conception, the embryo is about the size of a grain of rice, but already cells have developed which will form all the different parts of the body—blood, muscles, bones, skin, hair, and internal organs. A week later the embryo has doubled in size. It is now .28 inch long and its tiny heart has begun to beat.

At six weeks the embryo is just over .4 inches long. Its stomach, liver, and kidneys have formed and its head is beginning to develop. Its arms and legs are tiny buds. Two weeks later, at eight weeks, the eyes, ears, and even tiny fingers are forming, yet the embryo is still only 1.6 inches long—smaller than your little finger.

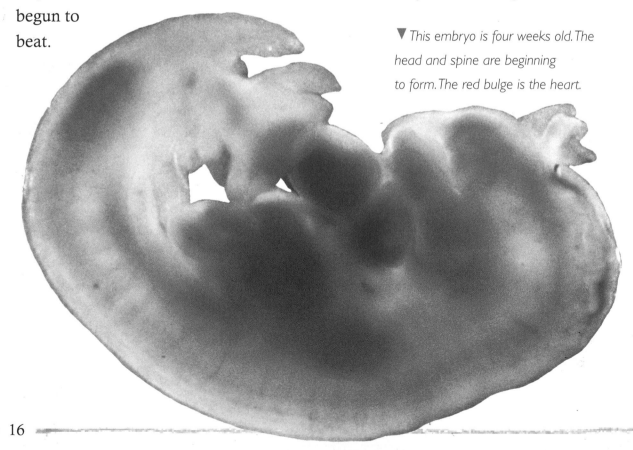

▼ *This embryo is four weeks old. The head and spine are beginning to form. The red bulge is the heart.*

◄ The embryo seven weeks after conception. The eyes are already forming. The head is huge compared to the body.

Capsule for survival

Only a few of the 64 cells that first reach the womb grow into the baby itself. Most form the **placenta** and a protective skin, or membrane, that makes a bag around the embryo and fills with **amniotic fluid**. The embryo floats in this liquid, protected from bumps and bangs. The placenta is a spongy lump connected to the embryo by the **umbilical cord**. The placenta allows food and oxygen from the mother's blood to pass along the cord to the growing embryo. It also takes waste away from the embryo's blood.

▲ This fetus is almost ready to be born. You can get an idea of its size by comparing its backbone with that of the mother.

Did you know?

The lungs begin to form when the embryo is just 7 weeks old, but it does not use them to breathe while it is in the womb. The lungs develop slowly and are filled with a salty liquid. While the embryo and fetus is in the womb, it gets all the oxygen it needs from the mother's blood. When the baby is born, the lungs have to pump away the fluid quickly and get ready to take in air.

Growing Bigger

At eight weeks the embryo is almost human-shaped, and from now on it is called a fetus. By the end of 14 weeks the body is fully formed, but it will spend another 24 weeks in the womb. In that time the fetus will grow bigger and its organs will mature, so that the body can survive after birth outside the womb. As it gets bigger, the mother's womb stretches to make room for it, and she becomes more and more aware of the fetus moving inside her.

The first kick

At 14 weeks the muscles are beginning to grow and, as they get stronger, the fetus moves its arms and legs more vigorously. But it is less than 5 inches long. It may be another six weeks before its mother can feel its feet kicking against her belly.

By then the fetus has doubled in size and the mother's womb is beginning to bulge. By six months the fetus would probably survive if it were born, although only if it were looked after in the protected environment of an **incubator**.

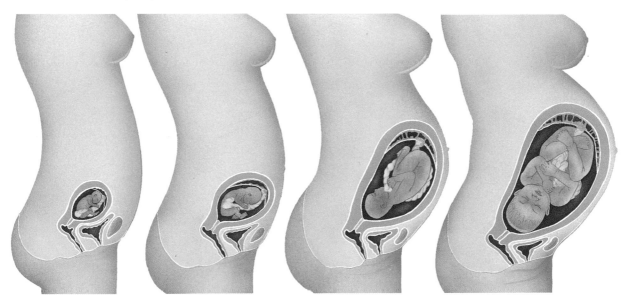

at 10 weeks fetus weighs about .6 oz

at 14 weeks fetus weighs about 5 oz

at 24 weeks fetus weighs about 25 oz

at 36 weeks fetus weighs about 7.5 lbs

▲ *A fetus grows more quickly than a human being does at any other time in life. The mother's womb stretches as its body grows.*

Life inside the womb

For the final three months in the womb, the fetus continues to grow stronger and put on weight. It sucks its thumb and becomes more aware of its surroundings. It can hear its mother's heart beating. It will even jump if there is a loud noise. From about 20 weeks, the fetus sleeps and can open and shut its eyes.

Its mother becomes increasingly aware of the fetus, too. Toward the end of her **pregnancy** she can feel its arms and legs moving, and she can feel it hiccuping! All this time the fetus is supplied with food and oxygen from her blood through the placenta. By about the 38th week, the placenta begins to fail and the fetus is ready to be born.

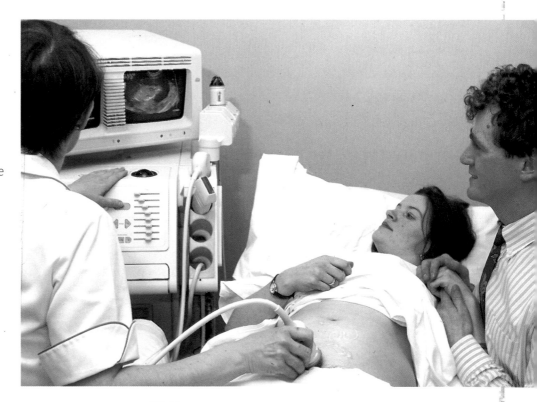

► This pregnant woman is having an **ultrasound scan.** She can watch her unborn baby moving inside her as the doctors check that the fetus is well and healthy. The machine uses sound echoes to make up the picture.

Did you know?

Anything in the mother's blood can pass to her fetus through the placenta, including the poisons of cigarettes and drugs. When a mother smokes, the fetus is deprived of vital oxygen. This can affect its mental and physical development. Fetuses can even become addicted to drugs.

Giving Birth

A mother becomes increasingly heavy and uncomfortable towards the end of her pregnancy. She can't wait for the birth. Giving birth is called labor and it is hard work for the mother. The womb, which is largely made of muscle, contracts to push the baby out. But first the cervix has to stretch to allow the baby through into the vagina.

First signs

A week or two before labor, the fetus usually turns in the womb so that its head is facing down toward the cervix. Often the first signs of labor are increasing spasms of pain in the belly, rather like menstrual cramps.

The pains are caused by the cervix slowly stretching. The cervix can take 10, 12, or even 18 hours to open fully to a diameter of 10 cm (about 4 inches), and during that time the pain becomes more and more intense.

► This baby is ready to be born. The cervix, which is still tightly closed, will stretch and open to allow the baby's head through.

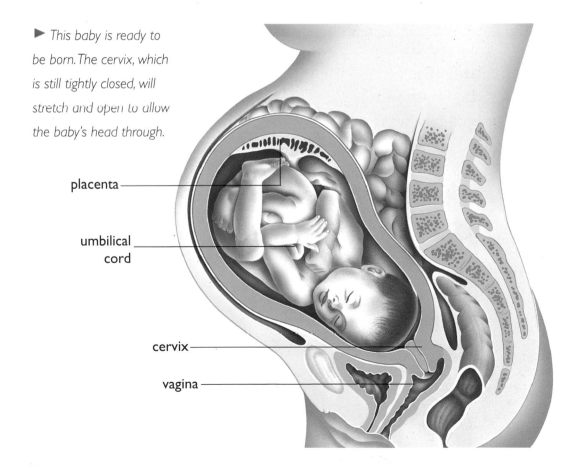

placenta

umbilical cord

cervix

vagina

Labor and delivery

Most women prepare for childbirth by practicing breathing and relaxation exercises to help them cope with the pain. If the pain is too great, however, there are different kinds of painkillers to help them. These are given by a midwife or doctor.

Pushing the baby out

When the cervix is fully open, the muscular walls of the womb begin to contract. Slowly the baby is pushed through the cervix and into the vagina, which stretches easily to let it through. The mother helps by pushing hard as the womb contracts. This stage of childbirth is shorter—usually an hour or less. Once the baby's head has emerged, the rest of the body follows easily. The baby has been born! The birth, however, is not over until the placenta has been pushed out, too.

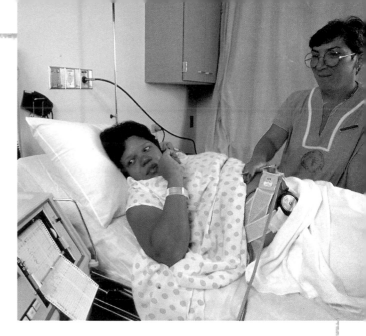

▲ A machine **monitors** the baby's heartbeat as labor progresses.

Did you know?
Many babies and mothers used to die from infections and complications. Today, midwives and doctors monitor the fetus and mother and take action if problems arise. Some babies are born by **Caesarean** section. A cut is made into the womb and the baby is lifted out.

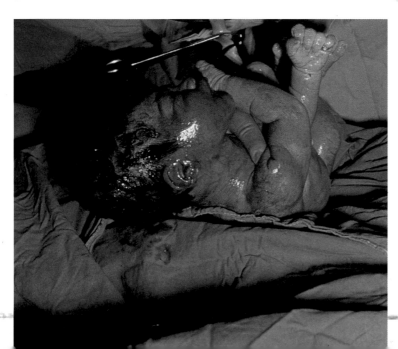

◄ This baby has just been born. The umbilical cord is still attached to his mother.

A Newborn Baby

It must be a big shock to a baby to leave the warmth and comfort of the womb and find itself in the world outside. It is almost totally helpless and must rely on others to look after it, but it is equipped with several **instincts** and **reflexes**. Some of these, such as sucking and swallowing, help it survive, but others, like jerking its arms and legs when it hears sudden noises, seem irrelevant and do not last long.. Because a newborn baby's neck muscles are not strong enough to hold its head erect, care must be taken when holding it.

The first cry

As soon as the baby is born, an amazing thing happens. It opens its mouth, takes a gasp of air, splutters, coughs, and cries! Up until now the lungs and breathing tubes have been full of fluid. Now the lungs no longer make fluid.

Instead, they absorb it and get ready to take in oxygen from the air. As soon as the baby has started breathing, the midwife or doctor clamps the umbilical cord and cuts it. The baby is now surviving on his or her own for the first time.

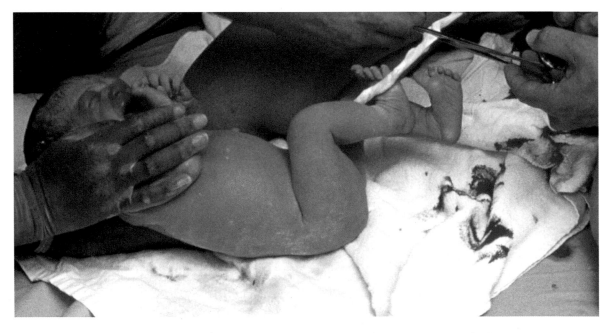

▲The umbilical cord is clamped and cut. It must be kept very clean until it shrivels and falls off naturally, about a week after birth.

The first meal

Both the mother and baby are ready for breast-feeding. The baby has a strong instinct to suck and will feed from the mother's breast. During pregnancy the breasts become larger and get ready to produce milk. As soon as the baby begins to suck, a cloudy, nutritious liquid called **colostrum** begins to flow. Within a few days it is replaced by milk.

Reflexes

A reflex is something you do without thinking. If something touches your eyelashes, you automatically blink. Newborn babies blink, sneeze, and swallow automatically. They also have several reflexes that don't last more than a week or two. For example, if you put a finger in each of the baby's palms it will grip so tightly you can pick it up by lifting your hands.

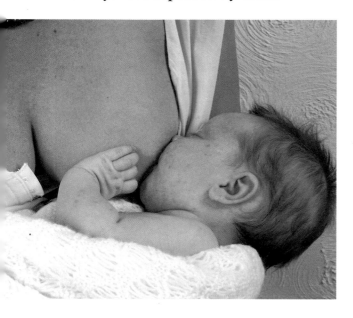

◀ *Babies suck automatically. Breast milk has all the nourishment they need. A baby also loves the warm comfort of a cuddle.*

Did you know?
All babies are born with blue eyes. Their eyes may change to brown within a few hours but sometimes it takes longer—several days or weeks. Some babies are born with hair on their heads, others are bald. A few are even born with a tooth.

▼ *A newborn baby's tiny fingers can grip surprisingly tightly.*

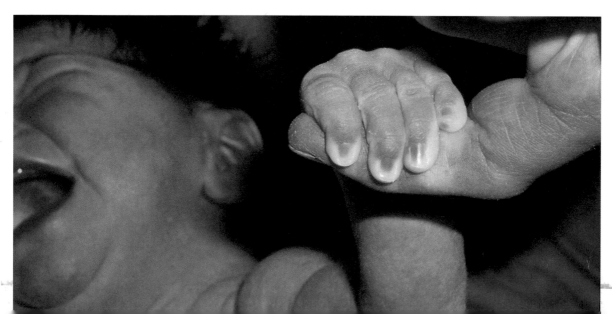

More about Chromosomes

The chromosomes that you inherited from your parents determine what you look like and whether you are a girl or a boy. Chromosomes are made up of **genes** and they carry coded information that tells the cells how to grow. The code includes directions about your sex, the color of your hair and eyes, and the shape of your body.

A boy or a girl?

Body cells contain 46 chromosomes, but sex cells (eggs and sperm) have only 23 each. When an egg and sperm join, the new cell has 46 chromosomes. There are 22 matching pairs and one pair which sometimes matches and sometimes doesn't. This pair carries the coded information that makes you a boy or a girl.

Girls always have two matching chromosomes shaped like an X, but boys have one X chromosome and one chromosome which is shaped more like a Y. While all female eggs carry an X chromosome, some sperm carry a Y chromosome and some an X chromosome. So the sex of a child is determined by the father's sperm.

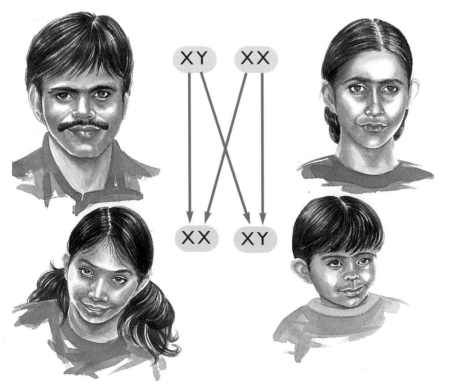

◀ *Follow the arrows to see how a boy inherits an X chromosome from his mother and a Y chromosome from his father. Girls always inherit and pass on X chromosomes.*

Dominant features

Every chromosome contains two instructions for every characteristic, one from each parent. Sometimes both instructions work together. At other times, one instruction overrules the other. If you inherit a gene for brown eyes and a gene for blue eyes, your eyes will be brown. Yet both parents may have brown eyes, but carry a "hidden gene" for blue eyes. If their child inherits this gene from both parents, he or she will have blue eyes.

◄ Can you see what each child has inherited from the parents?

Did you know?
Henry VIII of England was determined to have a son to succeed him as King of England, but his wives kept giving birth to girls. He divorced two wives and executed two because they had not "given" him a son. If only those wives could have told him it was he who had failed to produce a cell with a Y chromosome — so it was his problem all along!

Multiple Births

Twins are two fetuses who grow in the womb at the same time and are born within a few hours or days of each other. It can be quite confusing to meet two people who look exactly the same — which one is which? But not all twins look alike, because twins are formed in two different ways, producing identical or fraternal twins.

Identical twins

Chromosomes are inherited coded instructions that make sure each one of us is different from anyone else. If a single egg or cluster of eggs splits soon after fertilization, the resulting embryos have identical chromosomes. This means that the twins will be of the same sex and will look alike. Even identical twins, however, are not exactly the same and their families can always tell them apart.

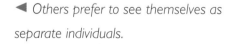
▲ Some identical twins like to emphasize the things they have in common and dress the same.

◄ Others prefer to see themselves as separate individuals.

Identical twins do have a lot in common, though. They often have the same mannerisms, likes, and dislikes. Some twins claim to know what the other twin is thinking, and to feel pain when the other is hurt.

Fraternal twins

Usually only one egg is released from the ovaries when a woman **ovulates**. Sometimes, however, a woman may release two eggs in the same month. If both eggs are fertilized, then she will give birth to fraternal twins. Fraternal twins do not have the same chromosomes.

They are no more alike than any other brothers and sisters. They can be a girl and a boy, or the same sex. Twins occur about once in every 89 births and they tend to run in families. But in the United States the number of pregnancies resulting in twins has been steadily rising.

▼ These **sextuplets** include two sets of identical twins. Can you spot them?

Nature or Nurture?

No one has a **personality** quite like yours. How did you come to be the person you are? Was it written in your genes, like your height and hair color? Or did your **environment** shape you? This is known as the question of nature versus nurture. Most scientists believe that both genes and environment help to shape the personality.

What is personality?

Your personality is the pattern of what you say, do, think, and feel. No two people have the same personality, but different people may have the same **temperament,** or general way of reacting to the world. Some people, for example, are outgoing, and others, shy.

The role of nature

Genes play a large role in determining personality. Identical twins, for example, have the same genes, and scientists find that identical twins grow up with much the same sense of humor, skills, and interests—even if they were raised apart.

The role of nurture

What you're taught, however, also affects your personality. There may be poetry in your genes, but your environment decides whether you'll write it in English or Chinese. Other people teach you language, as well as ideas, beliefs, and values.

◄ Even though two children are born into the same family, they may grow up to lead completely different lives. Environment, as well as genes, plays an important role in shaping a person.

Basic patterns

The basic patterns of your personality are probably set in early childhood when nature and nurture work closely together. In those years you have needs that come from nature, such as food, warmth, and love. Your environment decides how those needs will be met. Your temperament affects how you react to the care you get.

◀ *Nature and nurture working together will braid the unique personality of this child.*

Did you know?

Many psychologists think that the personality reflects a person's early family life. They believe that much mental illness and unhappiness in adults can be traced back to problems they never solved as young children.

Glossary

Abdomen Part of the body we sometimes call the "tummy." It includes the stomach, liver, and other organs, including the sexual organs.

Addicted Having a craving for something, such as cigarettes or drugs. Some substances are **addictive**. After taking them for some time, the body cannot do without them.

Amniotic fluid Liquid that surrounds the developing embryo and fetus in the womb and protects it from bumps and bangs.

Bladder Part of the body where urine is stored before being excreted from the body.

Caesarean section Operation in which the muscular wall of the womb is cut and the baby removed.

Cell Smallest living unit. Each part of the body is made of a different kind of cell.

Cervix The lower end, or neck, of the womb. It joins the womb to the vagina.

Chromosomes Tiny strands of chemicals found in the nucleus of each cell. They carry the coded instructions that tell the cells what to do. Chromosomes are inherited from the parents through the sex cells and make every individual unique.

Colostrum Cloudy liquid formed in a mother's breast in the first few days of breast-feeding.

Conception The moment at which a female egg and a sperm join together to produce the first cell of a new individual.

Embryo A developing baby from the first division of cells until all the main structures have formed. In humans this is the first eight weeks after conception.

Environment The surroundings, condition, and outside forces that affect a human being or other living thing.

Epididymis A tube next to the testicle where sperm are stored.

Fallopian tubes Narrow tubes that carry eggs from the ovaries to the womb.

Fertilization The joining together of a female sex cell and a male sex cell. An egg (female sex cell) must be fertilized before it can grow into a new individual.

Fetus The unborn baby from eight weeks after conception until birth.

Foreskin A fold of skin that covers the tip of the penis.

Genes Parts of the chromosomes. They carry information about inherited characteristics.

Hormones Chemicals produced by the body to control various processes. Sex hormones control the release of the eggs from a woman's ovaries and the production of sperm in a man's testicles. Female sex hormones also control the changes in a woman's body during pregnancy and birth.

Incubator A special cot for babies who are born too early. The incubator keeps the baby at a constant temperature and monitors its breathing and heartbeat.

Instinct Behavior that is present at birth — it does not have to be learned.

Membrane A thin layer around each cell that allows food and oxygen to enter the cell and waste to leave it.

Menstruation The process by which, once a month, the lining of the womb and the unfertilized egg leave the woman's body in a slow flow of blood.

Monitor To keep a continuous record so that problems can be detected immediately.

Muscle Bundles of fibers that contract (shorten) to produce movement.

Nucleus The central part of a cell, which contains chromosomes and so controls what the cell does.

Organ A part of the body which does a particular job. The purpose of the sexual organs is to create new life.

Ovary The part of a woman's body where the sex cells (eggs) are stored and where some female sex hormones are made. There are two ovaries.

Ovulate To release an egg from one of the ovaries. After puberty a woman ovulates about once a month until she is about 50 years old. Ovulation stops during pregnancy.

Personality The characteristic patterns of thinking, feeling, and behaving that set one individual apart from others.

Placenta An organ made by the embryo that allows food and oxygen to pass from the mother to the developing fetus without their blood coming into contact. It also takes waste from the fetus's blood to the mother's blood.

Penis The part of a man's body through which sperm and urine leave the body.

Period See **Menstruation.**

Pregnancy The time during which a woman carries an **embryo** and **fetus** in her womb. Her body goes through various changes to accommodate the growing embryo and fetus.

Puberty Period of time during which human beings become capable of reproducing sexually.

Reflex Automatic reactions that you do without thinking.

Reproductive organs Organs in the body relating to reproduction. In men, they include the penis and scrotum; in women, it includes the vagina, cervix, and Fallopian tubes.

Reproductive system All the parts of the body which are used for reproduction (creating a new life).

Sex cell Sex cells are produced by the sexual organs to create new life. A woman's sex cells are tiny eggs produced in the ovaries. A man's sex cells are sperm produced in the testicles.

Sextuplets Six fetuses that develop in the womb at the same time and are born within hours of each other.

Sexual intercourse The process in which a man's erect penis is put into a woman's vagina.

Sperm Male sex cells.

Tampon Cylinder of absorbent material which is placed in the vagina to soak up the blood during menstruation.

Temperament A general attitude toward or way of reacting to the world.

Testicle The part of a man's body where the sex cells are manufactured and male sex hormones are made. A man has two testicles.

Ultrasound scan A process that gives a picture of a fetus inside the womb using sounds and their echoes.

Umbilical cord A tube that carries blood vessels which connect the developing embryo and fetus to the placenta. After birth, the cord is cut and it shrivels to form the navel, or bellybutton.

Urine Fluid containing waste material from the blood mixed with water.

Vagina The tube that leads from the cervix and womb to the outside of a woman's body.

Vas deferens A long, thin tube that connects the testicles to the penis.

Vocal cords Two bands of tough tissue in the throat that vibrate as you breathe out in order to produce sound.

Womb The part of a woman's body where a fertilized egg gradually matures into a fully developed fetus.

Index

abdomen 8
amniotic fluid 17

babies
    birth 4, 20–1
    cry, first 22
    eye color at birth 23
    growth inside the womb 4, 16–19
    newborn 22–3
bladder 10, 11
body fluids 10,11
body hair 6, 7
boys
    chromosomes 24
    puberty 6–7, 10
breasts 6, 23

Caesarean section 21
cells
    body cells 16, 17, 24
    cell division 4, 14, 15
    nerve cells 4
    sex cells 4, 10, 11, 12, 13, 24
cervix 8, 20, 21
characteristics, inherited 15, 25
childbirth 20–1
chromosomes 14, 15, 24–5, 26, 27
circumcision 11
colostrum 23
conception 12–13
contraception 13

drug addiction 19

eggs 6, 8, 9, 12, 13, 14, 24, 26, 27
ejaculation 10, 12
embryos 14, 16–17, 18, 26
emotions, developing 6, 7
environment 28

epididymis 10,11
erections 10
eye color 23, 24, 25

Fallopian tubes 8, 9, 12
family size 27
fertilization 8, 12, 13, 14, 26, 27
fetus 4,8,17, 18–19, 20–21, 22, 26

genes 24, 25
girls
    chromosomes 24
    puberty 6, 7

hair color 24, 25
Henry VIII of England 25
hormones 6

incubators 18
independence, asserting 7
instincts and reflexes 22, 23

labor 20
labor pains 20
love, expressing 13
lungs 17, 22

membrane 13, 17
menstruation (periods) 6, 8, 9
monitors 21
muscles 7, 10, 16, 18, 20

nucleus 14

organs 4, 6, 10
ovaries 6, 8, 9, 27
ovulation 8, 9, 27
oxygen 16, 17, 19, 22

painkillers 21
penis 6, 10, 11, 12
periods 6

placenta 17, 19, 21
population growth 5
pregnancy 19, 20, 23
prostate gland 11
puberty 5, 6–7

reflex 22, 23
relaxation exercises 21
reproductive system   8

scrotum 10
semen 10, 11, 12
seminal vesicle 11
sex of a baby 24
sextuplets 27
sexual arousal 10, 12
sexual intercourse 12, 13
sexual organs 4, 5, 6
    female 4, 8, 9
    male 4, 10, 11
sperm 6, 8, 10, 11, 12, 13, 14, 24, 28

teenagers 6, 7
testicles 6, 10, 11
twins 26–7

ultrasound scans 19
umbilical cord 17, 21, 22
urethra 11
urine 10

vagina 8, 9, 12, 20, 21
vas deferens 10, 11
vocal chords 7

womb 8, 9, 12, 14, 16, 17, 18, 19, 20, 21, 22, 26

Further Reading

Balkwill, Fran. *Amazing Schemes within Your Genes*. Minneapolis: Carolrhoda, 1993.

Ganeri, Anita. *Birth and Growth*. Austin, Tex.: Steck-Vaughn, 1991.

Wilcox, Frank H. *DNA: The Thread of Life*. Minneapolis: Lerner, 1988.